Midnight Coffee

Midnight Coffee

POEMS BY

EDWARD M. GEORGE

NewSouth Books
Montgomery

NewSouth Books
105 South Court Street
Montgomery, AL 36104

ISBN 1-58838-035-1
This book was also printed, in December 2000, in a signed limited edition, ISBN 1-58838-017-3

Design by Randall Williams
Printed in the United States of America

To

my wife Sherry,

my friends Bill and Beverly Gandy,

Joe Stahlkuppe, and Michelle Padgett,

and the memory of Danny's Diner.

Contents

The Less Said / 11

Friends / 13

Midnight Coffee / 14
1969 Remembered / 16
Remembering Ella / 18
The Chinaberry Tree / 22
Buddy Ray and the Devil / 25
The Joint / 27
Ode to Joe / 29
My Guru / 31
A Special Pain / 33
Jer-ree, Jer-ree / 35

Family / 37

Photo of a Young Woman on a Back Porch / 38
Picture of an Old Man on a Brick Street / 40
Mama's New Babies / 42
New Baby / 45
Big River / 46
Baby Blue Cadillac / 48
Jefferson and Union / 51
The Face, the Man, the Farmhouse / 53
Grandpa's Ashes / 55

Love / 57

When I Have a Moment / 58
Like a Cowboy / 59

Sweet Pain, Sweet Fever / 60

Near the Charles / 61

Beside Me – Warm / 64

Gently, Please / 65

Song of the Ages / 66

Close Encounter at Wal-Mart / 67

Where the Rainbow Ends / 68

Juliette / 70

The Beach / 71

The Letter / 72

Fourteen and Sixteen / 73

Something Precious / 75

The Girl at the Grocery Store / 76

Toward the Setting Sun / 77

A Fleeting Moment / 78

The Affair / 79

War / 81

Beware / 82

Nam '67 / 83

The Death Bird / 85

The Taste of Death / 86

Young and Stupid / 87

God Is Here, Now / 88

The Medal / 91

Life / 93

A Thought / 94

Crazy Old Women / 95

Dead Zone / 96

Acid Trip / 99

A Sterile Room / 100
The Town Is Mine / 101
Linoleum and Jazz / 102
At the Bar / 103
Blues Man / 105
The Old Indian / 107
The Blind Man / 109
Summer Morning in the South / 110
At the Filling Station / 113
Guvner George / 115
Slavery Is Slavery / 117
Midnight on the Delta / 119
The Rendezvous / 121
Saturday's Lady / 123
Random Thoughts / 124
It Makes You Wanta Scream / 126
Full Measure / 128
The Little Girl Inside / 129
The Playground / 132
The End of Time / 135
The Wages of Zen / 136
All That Glitters / 137

Death / 139

Like the Wind / 140
The Flame of Life / 141
Dead Junkie / 143
On Okinawa / 145
She Lies Alone / 146
Memphis, August 16 / 147
The Retirement of Ray "the Cat" Walker / 149
Resolution / 151

The Less Said

You've got to know the value
of what you don't play . . .
— THELONIUS MONK

The poet
he said
must be
as Monk to jazz.
The note not played,
the word not said,
is after all
where genius lies.

Friends

Midnight Coffee

It was twenty after three
and there once more were we
trying to find eternal truth
sitting in a vinyl booth
in an all-night diner,
being served by a waitress
with her best years behind her.

The usual suspects slunk through the doors
punks and drunks, and pimps and whores.
But they only added texture
and color to the picture
of our haven for the lost and weary
with their eyes and souls gone bleary
from every sort of human excess
with no regard for what comes next.

I don't know how many cups of midnight coffee
have been drunk by Bill and me
over the years of our affinity
for self-examination in the very wee
hours of the night, roaming empty city streets
while righteous folks were home asleep.

In our many nights of midnight coffee
there's no remembering all the things we
talked about—from women to war
to there's no way that we'd die poor
or leave no mark behind us
before the reaper could find us.

Now our midnight coffee talks have dwindled
but every one we have still kindles
all those same old pangs of wondering
that have always kept us pondering
what the hell is it all about
and how long will it be till we find out.

1969 Remembered

Try imagining a place
Where it's always safe and warm.
"Come in," she said,
"I'll give you shelter from the storm."
— BOB DYLAN

There we were,
the doped up,
dropped out
cosmic children of the sane,
sharing electric sex
in a pungent haze
to the pulsing
soundtrack of our lives.
A bloodshot FM deejay
murmuring Jack Black nonsense
in the middle of the night.

Oh, did we rant then
against the sins of man.
Our ethical posturing
on Nam and race such
that we had all the answers,
to even questions
no one asked but us.

Our moral outrage
finally forcing us
to hide our awful shame
in the warm, moist
nooks and crannies
of our young and slender selves.

Remembering Ella

They sat
his mother and he
in his Park Avenue
in what was once
the dirt front yard
of the tenant shack
where she spent
the first fifteen years
of her life.

The house is gone
except for remnants
of a brick chimney
and a concrete front step.

A battered mail box
riddled with rusty buckshot holes
sits on a crooked creosote post
next to the narrow two-lane road
where only one old pickup
had rattled by
since they'd been there.

He'd brought her
from the city

to where she hadn't
been for forty years
unready
to be reminded
of a painful childhood
of picking cotton
for pennies a day
wearing
flour sack dresses
sleeping three to a bed
on a chicken feather mattress
always a little hungry
always aching
to get away
to anywhere else.

She'd been silent now
for several minutes
as in her mind
she saw herself
and her mother
and a little neighbor girl
sitting on a porch
no longer there
shelling butterbeans
into a tin washtub
and humming softly
to themselves.

"You know
we never had grass
in the front yard

but we'd take a rake
and make patterns
in the dirt . . .
I don't know why
we did that."

"Ella
loved blackberries.
They used to grow
in that ditch
right down there."
She pointed
to a spot
just down the hill
from where they sat.

"I guess
we'd better head on
to the church.
I'm not sure
I remember
exactly where it is."

For several miles
there were only the sounds
of the air conditioner humming
and loose gravel
crunching under
their tires
on the road
to the Mt. Zion
Church of God.

And then
she said
"You know what's funny.
I had finally decided
to visit her
just last week.
I would have
brought her blackberries . . ."

"She always
loved blackberries."

The Chinaberry Tree

In front of our house
on Union Street
stood
a big chinaberry tree
that served us
in many ways.

It was the lookout tower
for our enemies
of the moment,
whether wild Indians
or outlaws
or a posse
or the Bracewells
who lived up the street.

It gave us ammunition
for our homemade slingshots
and amusement
when we could goad
an unsuspecting cousin
into eating one of the
godawful-tasting berries.

Then one day
a big yellow truck
pulled up
and three men
from the City
got out
and chainsawed
our chinaberry tree
into little pieces
and hauled it away.

We spent a good part
of several days afterward
sitting in the front yard
staring at the spot
where had stood
our chinaberry tree,
wondering what
had caused the City
to come and cut it into
about a million pieces.

It was years later
that my mother
finally confessed
to calling the City
and asking them
to cut down
our chinaberry tree

before one of us
broke his damnfool neck.

But by then
we had discovered
girls
and it didn't really
matter much
anymore.

Buddy Ray and the Devil

Of all the hell raisers
I grew up with
Buddy Ray
was the hellraisingest
of them all.
He was a walking death wish,
a self-described
"hundred and forty-five pounds
of hell, death, and destruction."

One Sunday
when we were racing
at the Clanton Drag Strip
Buddy Ray dropped
a handful of reds
into a pint Mason jar
of moonshine
and lost his mind
for a couple of days.

Right before
he passed out cold
his eyes rolled back
and he started twitching
real bad
and speaking in tongues

and walking in circles
and raising his arms
to catch clouds
and put them
in his pockets.

We wrapped him up
with duct tape
and took him home.

He woke up
thirty-six hours later
when a bolt of lightning
blasted through the wall
above his head
and struck the floor
at the foot of his bed.

And then
when the smoke cleared
there
at the foot of the bed
amidst a strong smell of sulfur
stood the Devil himself
stroking his goatee
and grinning.

The Joint

Do not feel so all alone.
Everybody must get stoned.
— BOB DYLAN

We were between sets
in the parking lot
of the Kowboy Klub
when he proudly lighted up
the giant joint
that with great ceremony
he'd pulled from the pocket
of his fringed leather jacket
looking like Dennis Hopper
in Easy Rider.

Grass won't hurt you, man,
he said,
irritated at my polite refusal
to share
the joint
that he was trying to hand me.

Come on, man,
he whined,
as again I shook my head.

I said *no, man;*
I don't need no dope.

You damn ignorant
republican pig.
You drink don't you.
This is no worse
than drinking.

I don't need any more
bad habits.
I've already got
sex, booze, rock and roll,
and Jerry Springer.

Maaaaan, he said,
his whole body shaking
in frustration,
except for the arm and hand
still extending me the doobie.

Then he took
an extra long hit
and held it in his lungs
until his eyes bugged
and he coughed it out,
and with his glassy eyes
trying to focus on me,
he said, *Maaaan, . . .*
maaaan, . . .
maaaan, . . .
What was I just talking about?

Ode to Joe

*The creative life! . . . Rocketing out into the blue,
mounting, soaring, rousing the angels from their
ethereal lairs, drowning in stellar depths,
clinging to the tails of comets . . .*
— HENRY MILLER

With flames in his bowels
and fireworks flashing in his brain
he sits there at the machine
to sculpt a monument to a moment
of blinding inspiration.

With his soul flashing red and yellow
and his heart pounding like a bass drum
he knows that his next words will unlock secrets
of a thousand years ago
and ring through the land
like the coming of God.

It's not that he wants to write,
it's that he has to,
but if he didn't take his mind out for air now
and then,
it would rot,
and he would go screaming down the street

hoping for death at the bottom of a sewer
full of yesterday's urine.

He would will his body to the buzzards
and his useless soul
to the crazy old lady across the street
whom he never could stand anyway.

He doesn't ask you to understand
why he's like this
because he could never understand
why you're not.

He just asks that you
let him go on living
and promises to stay away
from your daughter.

My Guru

And ye shall know the truth,
and the truth shall make you free.
                                        — JOHN 8:32

There were a whole bunch of us
sittin' around
deep in thought
transfixed
by the ancient Indian music
and the scent
of burning incense
searching for the Truth
when
a cold chill
ran through me
and my skin began to vibrate
like a sitar string
as I felt the edge of Truth
drifting toward me
and my soul and mind
and body
becoming one
with the light
of the Truth,
and the Truth was

that my guru
was the same guy
who had tried to sell me
a timeshare.

A Special Pain

I had been lucky.
I had two true friends.
But then things changed.

First Henry betrayed me
by dying at forty-eight
of a bad heart
no one knew he had.

Taking with him
all those memories
which he could retrieve
so precisely
of the young fools
we had been.

Then Leonard
betrayed me
by slowly going crazy
with all his recollections
torn and twisted
into unrecognizable shapes.

Or beaten into dust
by Thorazine
and Lithium

and whatever else
they had used
to disconnect him.

It's so lonesome now
that in gray still moments
I sometimes want to join them
in those dark places
to where
they took my life.

Jer-ree, Jer-ree

I got back to my trailer
after doing my last show.
The trailer park was empty;
I said "Where'd everybody go?"
On a plane, the landlord said,
headed for Chicago
where they're gonna be guests
on the Jerry Springer Show.
The woman who married her dog
then divorced him for a cat.
The lesbian whose lover left her
cause she'd gotten way too fat.
The woman who left her husband
to sleep with his best friend
who was married to her mother
who ran off with another man
who had just broke out of prison
and was strung out on cocaine
and was dealing drugs to midgets
so that he could go to Spain
where he'd have an operation
so that he could change his name
to Roberta.

JER-REE, JER-REE, JER-REE.

Family

Photo of a Young Woman
on a Back Porch

My father's mother
died young,
of what or how
I don't know,
long before my birth.

For reasons
known only to himself,
he never spoke
of her.

And sadly
now that I finally have
her photo
found in the attic
of my Uncle Arthur,
a sweet man
himself now gone,
there's no one left
whom I can ask
what she was like.

I stare
at the young
short-haired woman
leaning against
the back door,
and in her
faded pre-war face
I see hints
of my father
my sister
my brothers.

And in her cocky pose
belying
her plain cotton dress
I see myself.

Picture of an Old Man on a Brick Street

My father's grandfather
died
the week before
I was born.
But I'm convinced
he touched my soul
even though the picture
that I'd always kept
in my head
of him
was different
from the photo
just found
in a long-forgotten
family album.

Still, I'm glad
to finally
see the face
of the man
who used to scare my mother,
a teenager
from Deatsville
who'd never seen up close before

a big dark Syrian man
with quick black eyes
and strong Arab hands
only a few years
removed from desert horses.

She later found
of course
he was a good man
who gave her fresh fruit
and promised her
five hundred dollars
if I
his first-born great-grandchild
was a boy.

Mama's New Babies

Her children
long grown and gone
my mother has adopted
the squirrels and birds
that frequent her back yard
to fight over
the bird seed in the feeder
hanging from the oak tree
or the scraps of bread
that she sprinkles about.

Or to splash in the water
in the concrete birdbath
that Danny bought her.

On the days when she sleeps in
her babies
squeak and squawk
their disapproval
over breakfast being late
till she gets up
in her faded pink housecoat
and fuzzy shoes

and tears and scatters
onto the damp grass
pieces of toast
getting her feet wet
but smiling
as they pounce
on the bits of bread —
the squirrels with their little leaps
the birds with their Charlie Chaplin strut.
She's gotten to where
she can recognize
the birds and squirrels
and notice when one shows up
for the first time.

She doesn't care when
I kid her
that the word is out
on the animal grapevine
that she's an easy mark.

On hot days
she checks to see
if the birdbath
needs refilling
so as not to leave
a bird
without a place
to clean its feathers.

She talks about
how the little birds

will wait
until the big ones finish.

She fusses about
a certain blue jay who
likes to splash the water
with his wings
and how when he's around
she has to fill the bowl
three times a day.

We gave her
a color picture book
so that she can look up
the different birds
and quit asking us,
who can barely tell
a robin from a bald eagle.

Sometimes when I come by
I catch her
sitting in a kitchen chair
nose against the back screen door
bread in hand
waiting.

New Baby

Four hours old
all pink
and wrinkled
with just a tuft
of fine blond hair.

Swimming toward the sky
with chubby little hands
cupping the air
until I give him my finger
which he clutches
with surprising strength.

Such a wonder he is
this tiny person
who even this early
in his tenancy on earth
seems ready
to get on with it.

Big River

I remember the river
    the wide river
        sometimes blue
        and sometimes brown
It brought the country folks to town
        carried cotton
        carried wood
        carried people
        bad and good
Carried preachers
        gamblers, too
            from New Orleans
            to ol' Saint Lou.

It cooled us on those summer days
        when even the air seemed to be ablaze.

It gave my father life's work to do
        and took my brother at the age of two.

It sometimes flooded our little farm
        but left good soil where it did its harm.

It's been a while
        bout thirty years
                since I left the Delta
                        streaming tears

But when everything's still
        and I'm all alone
                I think of that river
                that once was home.

That big, wide river that once was home.

Baby Blue Cadillac

I'll never get out
of this world alive.
— HANK WILLIAMS

North Union Street
Montgomery.
Christmas vacation
first grade.
I was sitting
on the front steps
sun on my face
when into our dirt driveway
drove a new baby blue Cadillac.

In our neighborhood
new baby blue Cadillacs
were as rare
as spaceships,
so I yelled, "Mama,
come look."
She was in the front room
ironing.

She got to the door
just in time
to see the car
drive off.
"You know who that was?"
she asked rhetorically.
"That was Hank Williams."

Hank Williams.
I knew the name
from the little pink plastic radio
Mama kept in the kitchen window
always on 740
the Big Bam.

Hank Williams.
From that day on
I listened closely
to the little pink radio
to hear
Hank Williams
on the Big Bam.
I liked his music.

But only a few days later
a man
came on the Big Bam
and in solemn tones
said Hank was gone
that he had died

on some lost highway
during the night
in the back seat
of the
baby blue Cadillac.

The silence of a falling star
lights up a purple sky.
And as I wonder where you are,
I'm so lonesome I could cry.
— HANK WILLIAMS

Jefferson and Union

I left something there
but when I went back for it
it was gone.
Time had taken it.

The streets were the same,
but they seem a little smaller
then when we used to race our bikes through
the stop signs
and one guy would signal us when to go.
We trusted him.

Progress had replaced
the house we lived in,
but the others looked about the same,
I guess,
but a little older and grayer
and not so much alive
as when we stayed up
till someone's mother
chased us off to bed.

There's a field of sand
and broken glass
where we played football,

risking life and limb
and maybe lockjaw.

The grassy spot
between the street
and the sidewalk
we used to wrestle on
and fake fights
to scare the people
driving by.

They've taken away the old streetlights
we used to shoot at with our slingshots,
but they left that tree stump
some drunk in an old Merc
ran into one night.

If you yell real loud,
it'll echo back
just the way it used to.
But it sounds kind of hollow
now.

The Face, the Man,
the Farmhouse

The face expressed a mind haunted
by yesterdays that were
and tomorrows that should have been,
a withered face.

The man stood on the edge of the ancient wooden porch
his faded overalls and khaki shirt still torn
from the barbed wire fence he'd stretched.
Bleary eyes peered down the long dirt drive
at the mailbox atop the creosote post.

The farmhouse was a simple structure,
frame with dingy white asbestos siding,
a dark green roof,
and a piece of wrinkled aluminum
that covered the leak near the chimney.

The face was lonely and still
as it recalled Sunday morning
and Betty Ann's vows to that Taylor boy
from Abbeville.

The man had lost a second daughter
to a life of wife and mother

that would make them strangers soon,
as it had with Joyce two years before
when she left with that soldier from Rucker.

The farmhouse was his alone now
with just memories
of the three most precious women ever.
"Why don't you remarry, Ben?" they'd said.
But who would marry a poor old dirt farmer like me?
he'd thought.

The face had moist eyes as Ben remembered Louise
and her promise of him a son
when the doctor told her
the next child would be the last.
She wouldn't say the first two times,
but she'd promised a boy the last.

The man clung to a cedar column
as he hung his head and softly wept
for the wife who had died bearing his lifeless son—
"When she found out, she gave up trying,"
was what the doctor said.

The quiet farmhouse welcomed him
into the kitchen for coffee
while the night wind blew through the pear tree
and the rain beat gently upon the wrinkled aluminum
that covered the leak near the chimney.

Grandpa's Ashes

When Grandpa died
they spread his ashes
over the garden
where he grew
the vegetables
that the family ate.

Love

When I Have a Moment

When I have a moment
I think of you.
It gives me peace
and makes the world
make sense.

Like a Cowboy

Do you love me?
she asked.
In my own way.
What does that mean?
she asked.
Like a cowboy.

She nodded
and smiled
as though
she understood.
She didn't.
But I was off the hook.

Sweet Pain, Sweet Fever

Silken union,
moist and steaming.
Time has stopped.

Pale honey drips —
envelopes us,
saturates us.
All is sweet.
Sweet pain, sweet fever.

Frantic nerves are laughing, crying.
Too bare to touch,
but don't let go.
Please.

Near the Charles

It was Valentine's Day 1967.
I was a poor soldier
from Alabama.
She was a rich girl
from Pittsburgh
studying ballet
at the Conservatory.

Somehow
our paths had crossed
and here we were
in Boston
leaving the theater
where we'd just seen
Blow-Up.
She understood it.
I didn't
but acted like I did.

I started to hail a cab
but she said don't
let's walk
it's not that far.
I said, girl,
it's twenty degrees

and snowing
and my Southern blood
is thin.

She said
I'll keep you warm
and hugged me
to her side
and kissed my cheek.
Her lips were cold
but soft.

Let's go see
if the river's iced over
she said
pulling me, shivering,
toward the Charles.

As we neared the water's edge
the snow increased
reminding me
of one of those
Christmas paperweights
with the
plastic snowflakes inside
falling
on a tiny Santa sleigh.

Look here
she said
falling backwards
into a pile of freshly fallen snow

flapping her arms
to make angel wings
and then beckoning me
to join her.

Leaving my senses
for a spell
I fell beside her
and made my own angel wings.

And then
she rolled over on me
and licked the snowflakes
from my chin
and kissed my frozen mouth
with hers.

Beside Me — Warm

A flick of a wrist
has killed the light.
It's night,
and I feel you now beside me—warm.

I lie still and stop my heart
to hear you breathe.

Gently, Please

Walk softly, Darling
       and smile sweetly
as you gently take the outstretched hand
       that pulls you here beside me
to take my body within yours.

Ecstasy sings softly
       as our bodies speak of love
and the world is dark and tender
       in the dampness of our minds.

Song of the Ages

Her smooth firm underbelly
smelled like a warm breeze
through a honeysuckle
and there was soft music
and little girl laughter
coming from the fine blonde hair
and the song
was the song of the ages.

Close Encounter at Wal-Mart

It had been thirty years
since I'd seen her,
and I wouldn't have recognized her
except that her dark gray eyes
were still like no others
I'd ever seen.

For just an instant
my heart banged against my chest
the way it used to
And then
she slowly walked away
without a hint of who I was

And I noticed that
just like me
she'd gotten old and gray
and fat and worn out.

And from then on
I hated her
for getting old and gray
and fat and worn out

And spoiling
the only dream
that I had left.

Where the Rainbow Ends

The lake lapped softly against the shore
and the smell of pine needles
and wildflowers
and your womaness
filled the summer air.

Your vanilla skin
glowed
in the moonlight
and your strawberry nipples
were ripe and sweet.

I wanted
all of you
with all of me
and you all of me
with you.

We ached to share
our outsides
our insides
our essences
our souls.

Our thoughts
swirled in such frenzy

that we couldn't tell
where yours began
and mine ended.

Naked in every way
we touched bare nerves
and traveled tender paths
we had never known
were there.

Until we reached that place
where time stops
and the rainbow ends
and the universe
converges.

Juliette

Her looks
were nothing special,
but her passion was.
She loved
like Janis sang,
with her guts
hanging out
and the
door to her soul
flung wide open.

But her allure
was yet her curse,
for in her wake
she left
the shell of
many a good man,
his innards consumed
by the flame
of her spirit.

The Beach

The sun betrays me
sitting on the same beach
that we owned for a while
one night.

The beach we walked
hand in hand
sometimes stopping
for an impulsive hug
and a kiss.

While the wind sang
and the ocean roared
the sand whirled around us
and your hair blew across my face.

While the moon peeped through the clouds
and the stars flickered silver
your hand traced my neck
and your heart pounded against my chest.

But, now, in the naked light
of early day
I see a barren beach
strewn with rusty beer cans
and I know
I'll never see you again.

The Letter

She's at her window
waiting
for the mailman
to bring a letter
from her love
who is off to war.

Across the street
I sit
at my window
and watch
and hope no letter comes.

Fourteen and Sixteen

Love is loveliest
when you're fourteen and sixteen
and holding her hand
makes you smile lewdly inside
cause it feels so warm and tingly.

You think you're one up on the world
cause she loves you and
you have someone to live for
to die for
if absolutely necessary.

You are so mature
that you can laugh at the child you were
last month
but your parents don't see it that way
they're too old, you see.

Marriage plans are discussed
with a solemn sincerity
and a definite finality
and you even call each other pet names

when there's no one else around
to snicker.

Ah
you face the world
with a newfound strength and conviction
and furrow your brow now and then
for your true love believes in you,
and love is everlasting
at fourteen and sixteen.

Something Precious

I was sixteen years old
sitting in the back seat
of Coy's black fifty-three Mercury hardtop.

The glasspacks were murmuring
and Skeeter Davis was singing *Something Precious*
on the radio.

All the windows were down
and the spring night air
was blowing through her hair
while she slept on my shoulder.

She smelled like shampoo
and innocence
and I smiled and wondered
if life could get any better than this.

The Girl at the Grocery Store

Our eyes met
and a warm shiver went through me
as I thought
how soft her cheeks must be
to touch
and kiss.

The suggestion of bare breasts pressed
against her T-shirt
and her jeans
were soft and worn
against the firmness of her thighs.

And then she smiled at me
and a warm rush
flooded my brain.

And then I sighed
and thought
to hell with it
and paid for my milk
and went home.

Toward the Setting Sun

Come sail away with me
she said so sensually
toward the setting sun;
tonight we'll lie under the moon
and the waves will sing their tune
and rock us both to sleep.
I'll keep you warm.

She had about her
a dark exotic mystery
of who or what she could be—
Arab? Spanish? Italian? Greek?
Was she a rich girl seeking fun
or just a whore running a con
on some unsuspecting geezer
who'd do anything to please her.

Try as I might, I couldn't tell.
So, I just said what the hell
and sailed with her toward the sun
and lay that night beneath the moon
and to the ocean's rhythmic tune
we slept.
She kept me warm.

A Fleeting Moment

Sometimes we are forever changed
not by those with whom we share our
lives but by one with whom we share
only a fleeting moment.

Like ships passing in the night
but not quite
they were.
Her silhouette
he can't forget
against the starlit evening fog
when she spoke in that low
voice to him
it resonated
something in his core
that never had before or since
been reached
or touched
except in secret dreams of her
that he'd not shared
nor dared
for fear they'd shatter
and the fragile pieces scatter
never to be found and bound again.

The Affair

And that is how we are. By strength of will
we cut off our intuitive knowledge from admitted
consciousness . . . which makes the blow ten times
worse when it does fall.
— D. H. LAWRENCE

I'd never before seen a man
deflate
so immediately
or completely
as did he
that day
when she told him
about the affair.

She begged his forgiveness
as she told him it was over,
that it could never ever
happen again.

But the pain on his face
was as though
his heart
had been ripped
still beating

from his chest
and rent to pathetic little pieces.

She
who had always been
so kind, so precious
had been with some man
whom he'd never seen
and wouldn't know
if he did.

She
without whom
he knew he could not live
had wounded him
in ways
that would not heal.

And even as he
held her so close
that their tears ran together
when he spoke of forgiveness,
he sadly knew
that he could never ever
fully trust her
again.

War

Beware

Know the enemy
and know yourself . . .
— SUN TZU

Beware of war
with enemies
who are not afraid
to die.

Nam '67

Red blood
flowing from an open wound.
Death screams
at the heat of noon.
Young men dying.
Young men dead.
When will enough be said
to stop
this fruitless, pointless dread
of sending our kin
to die in the night
so we can say
you're wrong—we're right.

How can we even claim
to be civil
when we glorify
this gory evil
of staining the stench
of jungle mud
with an endless stream
of human blood.

If reason prevails,
it won't be long
till we cease

this pseudo-righteous wrong
of slaying and maiming
in a fit of lust
to prove how much
in God we trust.

The Death Bird

Streamlined, sleek, and silver
the death bird comes screaming
back from the hunt,
tired and hungry but proud.

Its colorful plumage
of stars and stripes sparkle
as she comes to rest
smiling and panting.

Her smirk hiding
the horror of her latest victims,
spattered and scattered
in the jungle slime
their blood turning brown in the sun.

The gleeful screech
of the death bird still echoes in the minds
of those who speak of her fearsome splendor
while the funeral passes by.

Stand haughty now, death bird,
while they scrub and shine your wings
for the next hunt will be soon
and you'll go roaring off in glory
as the brass band plays
"God Bless America."

The Taste of Death

I tasted Death today
but savored life.
With combat's bullets
pressed against my heart and lungs,
I looked into the hollow pits of
Death's dark eyes
and saw life
looking back at me
from far away.

My flowing blood
drew Life to me nearer
till she stood tall at my feet
peering down into my soul
as if to seek the truth
that we both knew dwelt there.

And as she stood there staring
deep into my core, she knew.
And I knew.
And Death knew.
And Death turned his morbid head
and marched away
into a purple cloud
to wait another day.

Young and Stupid

He whose generals are able
and not interfered with by
the sovereign will be victorious.
— Sun Tzu

Sometimes I think of questioning
those who are wiser than me
Not because I disbelieve
but, to be reassured, you see.

I haven't been around for
very much or very long
so some of the things that they do right,
to me, seem slightly wrong.

God Is Here, Now

It's that time again
when here is there
and there is where
and God is dead
and living
in the hearts
of heartless, peaceful mongers
of merciful wars.

When black is white
and white is gray
and gray is black
and gray is white
and black is black
and God forbids
and God allows.

And then is now
and now is gone
and soon is late
and late is early enough
to be soon
now and then—
God is now
and then.

When far is near
and near is infinity
waiting around the corner
from maybe
and God knows—
but God is dead
and living.

When wrong is right
and right is right
only now and then
but then is now
and now is gone
and gone is here
and here is there
and there is where—
God knows where
but he ain't talking.

When fast is slow
and slow is swift
and swift is too slow
to be fast—
but God is fast
and fast is slow.

When round is square
and square is bent
too round
to be square—
but God is round enough
to be square enough

to be round enough
to be square.

When the word
is not the word
but another word
that sounds that way—
God has words
but they just sound that way.

Ah, some scream silently
at those who whisper loudly
that God is here, now,
but here is there
and now is gone . . .

The Medal

They took my brother away
and brought back
a purple heart.

A clump of metal
and a piece of rag

In exchange
for a boy
with laughing eyes
and a freckled nose.

Life

A Thought

When I was a child
my feet were bare upon the earth
and I walked with the wind
rather than against it.

Crazy Old Women

There were two
crazy old women
who lived in our neighborhood
and walked the sidewalks
carrying dog-eared bibles
and asking
Have you been saved?

They always wore black
and a clown-face
of makeup
and rumor was
that they used to be whores
before they got
old and ugly.

Dead Zone

It was three weeks after Uncle Sam
had loosed me from the Nam
and handed me my walking papers
and two thousand saved-up poker dollars
that I awoke from
a four-day drunk
in the floor of a tie-dyed school bus
with a skinny long-haired chick
who was pulling on a rainbow sarong
and mumbling some weird shit
about universal love and
how Jerry would forgive me
for killing Cong babies
if only I would tune in on the
love tone.

I held my head together
with my hands
and stepped off the bus
into a tie-dyed blur of
motley Manson wannabes
and acid-addled homely chicks
dressed up like clowns,
dancing like epileptic zulus
and singing off-key bullshit songs
about staying stoned

and how the world goes in circles.

Having no notion of where I was
or how I got there
I went back onto the bus to
sleep off the banging in my brain
and ask the rainbow girl
if I had married her or
joined some cult
or robbed a bank
or done some other dumb-ass thing
during the days my mind
was on vacation.

We love you, man, she said.
It was fate that brought
you to the Deadlot
for salvation from your
wicked ways.

She placed my hand
against her breast and
told me how broken her heart
would be if I did not see
the light shining
through the crack in
the cloud Satan
had placed upon my soul.

Then she pulled my head to her bosom
and told me how
if I would only give in to the music

it would cleanse
the bloodstains
from my head and heart.
I said, all right, okay, anything
just let me sleep off
this goddamn hangover.

Sometime during the night
an awful racket
blasted through the bus
and I dove for cover
thinking it was incoming
only then to realize
that it was the rainbow girl's love tone
that was pounding on my body.

The noise was more than I could stand
so I stumbled off into the dark
holding in a paper sack
all my stuff that I could find
among the clutter of the bus.
As I headed for the highway
I looked back to see
what appeared to be miles of
doped-up denim disciples
swaying to the rhythm
pulsing from the stage
where there was some
bearded fat guy
playing guitar loudly
and badly
but joyfully.

Acid Trip

A calliope
and balloons
pink and yellow
luminescent
take me away
from peeling paint
and murky dank
to Ferris wheels
and cotton candy
sugar white.

A Sterile Room

Through the window of her sterile room
she heard the song of the ice cream truck
and it took her from her sterile gloom
back to a place where she could tuck
her fears into a tiny pack
and stuff them in her back pocket
and ride them on a wooden horse
with cotton candy as their source of food.

A calliope pumping joyful noise
into the night and bringing boys and girls
their rightful share of freedom from
those frightful fears
that bring them tears and
put them here in sterile rooms
to sit and stare in sterile gloom
and softly cry into the night
and wonder why there is no light.

The Town Is Mine

When the night is old
    and the dew is young,
the town is mine
    as I stroll along the empty streets
and hear my footsteps echo.

I stuff my stiffened hands
    into my flannel pockets
and watch a star plunge to a fiery death
    in the cobalt sky
above the skating rink.

Linoleum and Jazz

Bird's notes
float through the smoke
hanging over the
linoleum table top.

My heel clicks time
against the
steel leg
of a red vinyl chair.

A hard blonde waitress
sets another Chivas
right where the napkin says
"Welcome to the
Blue Note Lounge."

At the Bar

I pour another drink at my glass
one more double shot
one more puddle on the naked table top.

Around the bar
I see:

Lost men

       with bleeding eyes
       in rough workclothes
       smiling at worn jokes
       cussing God and country
       and man and beast.

Empty-eyed musicians

       squeezing groans
       from aching horns
       beating moans from tired drums
       staring through stale smoke
       at nothing in particular.

Frumpy bar fly

       smiling vacantly
       at haggard husbands

hiding from nagging wives
and crying kids.

Lonely sailors
        drowning the hollow pain
        of homesickness
        and the monotony
        of monotony.

Fat, bald bartender
        with hairy tattooed arms
        wiping the formica bar
        for the millionth time
        listening to everyone
        hearing nothing.

Wino with matty beard
        at the end of the bar
        his knotty hand
        holding a shaky glassful
        of red poison
        sinking slowly
        into the cool darkness
        of another place.

And
in the mirror
Me.

Blues Man

Oh, Lawd, yeah
dat blues man
he jus keep on wailin dem sorryfuls
an moanin dem blues
lack de sun ain gone shine no mo.

Yeah, baby
he be pattin dat foot
an bangin dat ole guitah
to beat all hell.

Eyes haff shut
an head bobbin up an down
rollin side to side
he be groanin bout dat gal
who leff him all alone
an dem twenny years he got to go
in dat lonesome prison cell.

He be cryin bout dat card game
down in Nawlins
an how his heart ache
when dat lonesome whistle blows.

He be grinnin bout dat big fine lady
wid de big fine laigs

an recollectin bout dat sherrif
who done chased him outta town
an how hot it gits in dem cotton fields
when de sun gits high.

Den, Lawd,
dem blues gits in yo blood
and fore you know it
you be pattin yo foot
an snappin yo fingas
an achin an moanin
rat along wid de blues man
wid de Bogart hat
an de salt an peppa hair.

An den fore you know it
he be singin his lass song
bout dem golden gates of glory
an praise be de Lawd
an you just kinda pull yo hat down ovah yo eyes
an put yo hands in yo pockets
an sorta slip away
hummin bout de big fine gal
wid de big fine laigs.

The Old Indian

This was the first time I did not believe
in the "reality" of my perception . . .
                              — CARLOS CASTANEDA

Sitting on a wooden bench
on the porch of an old store
on a back road to Albuquerque,
his ancient Indian eyes
were as calm
as a summer lake.

He smiled slightly
as I stared
at his weathered face,
its skin favoring
a well-worn
catcher's mitt.

You have a good spirit
he said
as I walked inside.
Then he closed his eyes
and dozed off,
his arms across
his faded denim shirt.

When I came out
just moments later
I turned to say good-bye,
but he was nowhere
to be seen.

I looked all around
but saw nothing
but desert and highway.
I even peeked around back
just in case
he was pulling
some Castaneda thing.

I looked back
one last time
as I drove away
and got a chill
as I wondered
if I had imagined him.

The Blind Man

He said
you know
in my dreams
I can see again.

Sometimes
I wake up
and cry.

Summer Morning in the South

In the country
    a crinkled leather face
        peers squinty eyed
        toward the rising sun
            at rows of melons
                to be loaded up today
                    for sale in the city.

Little boy inside stirs
        at first light of day
    yellow shaggy hair haloes brown freckled
        innocence
    worn out ball glove hangs off one bed post.

Lazy hound yawns
    and walks slowly away from Morpheus
        to be at his master's side
        for a morning scratch on his canine skull.

In the kitchen
    the smell of fresh coffee
        hot biscuits
    "Jesus Loves Me" hummed in
        soft feminine tones
    clink of plates being set
        upon a sturdy wooden table.

In the city
      constant buzz hum roar
            of ever present air conditioners
      birds bidding the world good morning
            in high, shrill songs
      a car
            now and then
            breaks the silence.

      the paper boy throws headlines
            and comics
                        onto a porch here
                        and there

      soft thud
      as latent news falls
      waiting to be read.

      clink clink roar
      the milkman's come and gone.

      a baby cries out
            awakened by nightmares
      young mother stirs
            and comes to life.

Soon the city will be awake and bustling
      and talking
                and selling
      and arguing
                and agreeing

and playing
            and fighting
and a few busy shoppers
        will quickly stop by the
                    farmers' marker
                        to buy a melon
                            or two.

At the Filling Station

It's all right
working late at night like this.
Everything's so quiet now,
that I just get up
maybe once an hour—
Yankee tourists coming in
"fill it up—
I'm in a hurry."
Yankees are always in a hurry.

The coke machine's cheated me
out of three dimes tonight,
but I made it up on a can of oil
30 cent oil for 60 cents.
They don't know the difference—
suckers for tv ads
"our oil is good stuff—
just watch these beakers."
Big deal.

Damned old Elroy
keeps coming around.
Smells like muscatel.
He thinks I don't know
he's looking for a chance
to walk off with something.

Crazy Elroy,
always wearing short-sleeve shirts.
Wine keeps him warm
I suppose.

My car sure looks great
since I've been working here.
All clean and waxed up.
Needs a tire though.
Maybe next week.
Date with Hazel this week;
god, she's sweet.

Suppose I oughta wash down the front.
What the hell, do it later.
Looks better if I wait till almost morning.
All the paper and dirt washed into the street.
What the hell people wanta drop stuff
a foot from the trash can for I don't know.

One of these days
I guess I'll go back to school
get some nice clothes,
a good job somewhere.
Trade off my car.
I guess I can't work here all my life
pumping gas.
Specially when somebody comes in
in a big car
and looks at me like I'm stupid.
Know what I mean.
Moon sure is pretty tonight, though.

Guvner George

It was hypnotic
the way the little man
behind the podium
on the flatbed trailer
spoke about how
we had to stand up for our rights
and not bow down
to the Federal guvmunt
or judges who had no respeck
for the common man.

His small fist
first pounding the podium,
then flailing in the air,
you could almost see sparks flying
from his piecing eyes
as he railed about
how we were just as good as anyone
and tired of being treated
like we didn't count for nuthin.

As the crowd went crazy
in the Alabama hell heat,
he wiped loose strands
of dark, oily hair
from his forehead

and proudly took in
the effect that he was having
on us poor souls
who, before him, had no commonality
except our insignificance.

As the frenzy quelled,
he loosed his skinny black tie
and the top button
of his short-sleeve white shirt
and solemnly assured us
that for as long as he drew breath
our little children
would never have to share
classrooms with nigra children
because that's not
what either race wants.

I had never in my young life
seen folks so fired up
as when he wound up his speech
to the sound of a country band
who played him off the trailer
and into a black Buick
that sped away
to another courthouse square
in another rural county
where he would weave his spell
and forever change the meager lives
of those of us theretofore untouched
by the winds
of political storms.

Slavery Is Slavery

I wonder if ever there will come a day
when my black brothers
will tear free from
the strings
pulled by those
who profit most from their
despair.

When they will realize
that it is not freedom
to exchange
chains of steel for
chains of empty promises
and catchy slogans.

When they will recognize
that massah is now called Reverend
and wields not a whip
but clever words
to hold them hostage
to their lot.

When they will see
the disconnect
between themselves
and those who limo

with kings and presidents
and rest their diamond pinky rings
on arms of first-class seats
in transatlantic jets.

When they will understand
that to be spoken for
as one
is to have no say at all.

And it is not freedom
to overcome those who owned their bodies
only to fall subject to those
who would own their minds.

Midnight on the Delta

The tinted moon
backlit the fog
sitting in the skinny branches
of the barren Delta trees.

The only sounds
the grind
of tires
on the wet highway
and the rumble
of a long freight train
heading south
to Flora.

I turned off
the radio static
and cracked
the window
hoping the cold wind
would clear
my sleepy head.

But it seemed
that all I'd done
was make a way
for ghosts

looking to get warm
to climb inside
and plant
those weird thoughts
I always get
at midnight
on the Delta.

The Rendezvous

I can rarely hear a country tune
        and not think of the old café
down the street from my childhood
        where the plumbers and painters
and carpenters would gather after work
        to guzzle down a few beers
before they had to go home
        and face their drab wives
and their screaming kids
        fighting over which tv show
they would watch instead of studying
        for the school they would
drop out of anyway.

These men with no past, no future,
        and whatever present they could conjure up
would keep that country music pouring
        from the old jukebox with the glass
that was cracked in a fight
        three weeks ago.

On weekends
        they would be there with their
hair slicked back
        and their shiny new shirts

to drink themselves to oblivion
        and maybe drum up a piece
from the waitress
        for when after she got off.

Most of the time
        I was scared to go in there
but once in a while
        when it was kind of quiet
I would strut in
        and pick out a table near the jukebox
and listen to that good country music
        that kind of fit right in
with the mood of The Rendezvous.

Saturday's Lady

At dawn
a brazen lady
embellishes his bed—
A lady who for fifty dollars
did her magic tricks for him.

Who in the second-hand light of early day
is like a child asleep,
with red lips slightly parted
and not so bright
as when they spoke those words.

Her hair is loose and not so hard now
as it lies asleep against her blonde skin.
The pale blue veins and freckles on her neck
make last night's erotic fancy
a woman,
one who's come to be a part of him eternal
and taken him to be a part of her.

He contemplates her pallid profile
and wonders what tiny twist of fate
has lain her here beside him in his dismal flat
instead of in some Queen Anne bedroom
with the station wagon parked outside.

Random Thoughts

Random thoughts
ricochet in my head.
Try as I might
I can't seem
to line them up
in any kind of order.

And it's all
her fault.

I had made up my mind
to live alone
in peace
with my paint and my music.

To keep my soul and studio
creative,
clear of carnality
and frivolity.

Until that day
when she stopped in
asking for directions
to the interstate.

If only I'd
gotten her number.
Or at least
her name.

It Makes You Wanta Scream

Wading through the garbage and puke
searching for the end—
it makes you wanta scream
doesn't it
Hot and muggy
with your nose aching from the stench
and the gnats getting in your eyes
you wipe your face
with the back of your hand
but it tastes like shit
and it makes you wanta scream
but what the hell
nobody's listening.

Your legs ache
and you have to piss—
it makes you wanta scream
doesn't it
Sunburn aching
and your crotch rubbing raw
from the sweat and your wrinkled up shorts
you try to straighten them out
but it just aches more
and it makes you wanta scream
but you don't do it
cause it's too damn hot.

And you're thirsty
and your lips are parched—
it makes you wanta scream
doesn't it
Dust in your sweat
makes your face cake up
and your fingers feel dirty
and don't want to touch one another
cause it sends chills down your back
and you feel like shit
and you wanta scream
so you go ahead and do it
but what the hell
nobody's listening.

Full Measure

Your dreams
should always lay
just beyond your reach
so that you
have to stretch
to your full height
and
find out
how tall
you really are.

The Little Girl Inside

She was so smart
so sleek
so well turned out
as they congratulated
her success
that no one else could tell
that just below
that cool surface
lay demon memories
of daily dealing
with pangs of
raw poverty.

Sometimes homeless
always hungry.
Not one
decent dress.
The giggles of
classmates whose faces
she can't even remember
still hurt
as they echo
down the

concrete corridors
of a school
long torn down.

Many a good man
has tried to charm away
her icy serenity
not knowing
that it was their very charm
their flirty patter
their after shave
that opened doors
where inside lay
the smell of
hot beer breath
and the feel
of rough dirty hands
forcing young thighs apart
to violate her
so deep
that even time
can't heal the wound.

Even now
some nights
she wakes up
screaming,
streaming tears
and sweat.
Wiping away blood
from years ago.

Even now
some days
her mind strays
against her will
to fears
of someone,
something
taking that away
she's worked so hard
so long
to have
so as not to ever
ache again
of a vacant stomach
or feel the pain of
others viewing her
as a
lower form of life.

Even now
she trusts no one
except herself
to come into
that special place
where inside dwells
that ragged hungry
little girl.

The Playground

I never saw him coming.
His headlights were off
and he was too drunk
to hit the brakes
before he plowed into
the passenger door
like an angry bull
into a matador.

Next thing I knew
I was crushed
into the steering wheel.
A hot pain in my ribs
and blood gushing
from a slash
across my cheek.
I couldn't tell
if I was up or down.

And then
the pain was gone
and I floated
from the truck

into a long tunnel
toward a soft light.

And then
I was in the grass playground
of my first school
with my classmates
all around me
playing their children games
and laughing
their children laughs.

And then
I saw my grandma
walking toward me.
First time I'd seen her
out of her wheelchair.

I reached for her
and pulled her to me
and smelled
the grandma smell
of her apron—
coffee and apple pie
with raisins.

As I held her close
she said
You know you can't stay.
It's not your time.
When I kissed her cheek

I smelled the cold cream.
Then she was gone.

As I was pulled
from the playground
I saw Freddie Haynes
in his soldier suit
waving from a bench
beside a stream
telling me with his eyes
that everything was okay.

The End of Time

My thoughts stretch
across the crowded emptiness
of my mind as I am alone
yet claustrophobic
with the closeness of others—
as I realize
that my life
is but a flash of light
and a whimper of sound
in the three ring circus
of Time.

But to me
I am Time,
for each man to himself
is Time
and each man to himself
is Existence
for when he goes,
so shall the world go,
for him.

The Wages of Zen

Understanding
is not
a goal
to be achieved.

It is
instead
a gift
to be received.

All That Glitters

Don't confuse
rumor
with information,
or mistake
information
for knowledge,
or assume that
knowledge
is wisdom.

Death

Like the Wind

Most of us
come and go
like the wind.
Ruffling the leaves a bit
but leaving no mark
on the tree.

The Flame of Life

A striking girl,
she'd always been so strong
for someone so young
and slight.
So wise
for only seventeen
that it was hard for us
to realize
she'd never known before
how quickly
the wind of fate
can snuff out
even the brightest flame
of life,
without warning
or mercy . . .
or reason . . .

But now
I lay my hand upon her cheek
and in her eyes I see
a sadness
where only joy had been before—
A hint of hardness
where just yesterday
was only tenderness.

To her,
everything was certain
ironclad
until just hours ago.

But now she's learned
that growing up
is knowing there are things
that don't make any sense
and never will.

Finding out
that life
is just one damn thing
after another,
but still keeping the faith
and squeezing out
and savoring
every ounce
of juice there is.

Dead Junkie

They found his body
crumpled
in a heap
on the wet winter sidewalk.
His sunken eyes
wide open
but vacant
where once had been
joyous mischief.

His damp clothes caked
with city filth.
His body so racked
from crack and smack
till finally
even the old fags
who haunt the
back alleys
didn't want him
in their mouths.

His mother's cheeks
were streaked
with tears of grief
and yet relief
from wondering

where he was
and when
he might again
sneak in
and steal her checks.

She'd not slept
a full night
since she'd banned him
from her home
so as
not to wind up
with nothing of value
or maybe dead.

His ex
when they told her
just said yeah
and shrugged
and held their
baby tighter
and kissed him
lightly
on his little eyes
so full
of joyous mischief.

On Okinawa

Atop this rock,
        I hide
to catch the sand below
        being kissed
by the East China Sea.

The sky is black
        as black can be.
The stars are fiery pinpoints
        around
a werewolf's moon.

My mind looks
        across the rippling ink.
I see Confuscius.
        Ivory flesh.
Jade flutes.

It was here,
        three days ago,
two fishermen were washed away
        by the typhoon
never to be seen again.

She Lies Alone

Awake in the cold hospital bed
she cries
a child's tears
on the pillow
with two serpents
around the sword.

Thoughts
of tiny hands
against her face
a toothless laugh
that dribbles
the name she won't need now
haunt her
as she lies alone
with her arm across her flat stomach
wondering why.

Memphis, August 16

I'll never let you go 'cause I love you so
so please don't ever say good bye.
                                    — ELVIS PRESLEY

"Just three weeks ago he was seen in Provo
by a woman who his mother used to know."
This bit of news was told to me with scary sincerity
by an old lady in tight white satin shorts
and a T-shirt that reports
"Elvis lives."

"He's lost about forty pounds or so,"
she must have thought I ought to know,
and so I smiled and nodded back
"and he's kept his hair jet black.
And you know he still looks great
even with that beard that hides his face."

I was getting really nervous when
we were joined by two fat men
in leather pants and leather hair
who told me that they were there
because a gypsy that they knew
had told them Elvis would be due

back home to Graceland any day
to tell us why he'd been away
and promise he was back to stay.

"It's all about aliens and the CIA
the reason that he went away,"
the woman whispered to me
as she looked around to see
if there were any suspicious minds
in the long, patient lines
waiting to make the yearly pass
through the portals of the Master's last
earthly palace, a place where
for one fleeting moment mere
common folks can share the glory
and revel in the mystic story
of how one of their very own
had shown them all
and come to be known
as "The King."

The Retirement
of Ray "the Cat" Walker

A forty-year-old
right fielder
batting two-sixty
in Class A ball.
Going nowhere,
been nowhere.
But he couldn't let go
of the game.

The warm Florida sun
on his face.
New-mown bermuda
under his cleats.
The clack of a new white ball
hit square by
northern white ash,
then snapped out of the air
by his Rawlings Pro-6.
These things
were in his blood.

Barely hanging on
to a spot
better filled
by a nineteen-year-old phenom,

he couldn't let go
of the game.

Three ex wives
and four children
got about all he made.
But when he was standing
in front of the Budweiser sign
peering into the plate
to pick up the ball
off the bat,
it didn't matter,
because he still had the game.

It was the day after
Skip told him
that they were
cutting him loose
that he walked off
into the Gulf
in full uniform—
his Pro-6
strapped around
the Louisville Slugger
on his shoulder.

Resolution

As he held his father's hand,
he felt the life force leaving
the riddled remains
of a man
who had in life
been so soft and pitiful
but was in death a rock,
not giving an inch to pain
or the imminence of his demise.

He only wished they'd made amends
for all the feuds they'd had
which seemed so silly now.
But, in his heart he heard the tolling bell
and knew that he'd be forever doomed
to bear the weight of words unspoken
and the ache of tensions unresolved.

And then he felt his father's hand
squeeze his
and compel him closer
before the old man
softly coughed and gasped
and smiled and left.

ED GEORGE is a Montgomery, Alabama, attorney
and education management consultant who likes to
try his hand at poetry and songwriting when he's not
playing softball or tennis. This book is his first
collection of poetry and includes poems written over
a period of about thirty years.

www.ingramcontent.com/pod-product-compliance
Lightning Source LLC
Chambersburg PA
CBHW022010090426
42741CB00007B/967